YouTube Sponsorships:
How Creators Like You Can Fund Your Channel

By Carey Martell

YouTube Sponsorships: How Creators Like You Can Fund Your Channels
First Edition, 2015
All rights reserved.

ISBN-13: 978-1530384679
ISBN-10: 1530384672

More books by this author:
http://martellbooks.com/

Author's personal blog:
http://careymartell.com/

TABLE OF CONTENTS

Introduction

A sponsorship deal is not free money. It is a business transaction where the company is purchasing a service from you and expects to obtain results.

Each year companies spend $17 Billion on sponsorships. In particular, the music industry spends $1.17 Billion on sponsorships each year. This is an ideal source of funding to tap into for any music oriented YouTube creators.

However, many video bloggers simply have no idea what a good sponsorship deal is. They do videos for either low or no money that, if they were more knowledgeable, would have earned them six figure deals.

Sport athletes and film actors don't do endorsements for free. Why should you?

Mostly it comes down to overcoming the mental barrier that many creators imprison themselves in; the extremely naïve and self-defeating attitude that they either don't deserve to be paid for their work or that doing so will somehow make them a horrible person. Some even delude themselves into believing they will have no "freedom" if they accept a brand's deal on their terms, even though the work will only consume a few days or weeks of their time.

If you are a popular YouTube creator and you have an attitude like this, you should seriously re-evaluate your perspective. Once you let go of this self-defeating mindset you can change your life almost overnight.

What Are Sponsorship, Endorsements and Partnerships?

Although people often confuse these for being the same thing, they are actually quite different:

- **Sponsorships** are an advertising tool utilized by a brand where they purchase some or all of the costs involved with a show or film in exchange for the brand to be featured in the project. The Sponsors goal is to become connected with projects that will be watched by the audience.

- **Endorsements** are a situation where a celebrity openly states that they recommend or suggest that someone else use a specific product or service. The Sponsors goal is to generate sales by using a celebrity's influence.

- A **Partnership** is a business deal between legal entities (such as a studio, a brand and a distributor) and in the context we're discussing, would be for development of a new show, film or other entertainment product. Often a new company (usually a limited liability company, or LLC) is setup specifically to be the owner of the intellectual property of the project, and each company holds a % of ownership in the new company.

Why Bother? Isn't YouTube Ad Revenue Enough?

Many YouTubers, due to their inexperience with the traditional media industry, do not understand the motivations of brands. It is beneficial to find a manager who can assist you with these deals to represent your interests.

Brands hire ad agencies to churn out commercials and endorsements as part of a shotgun blast approach to marketing. The only long-term brand endorsers are those actors who play company mascot characters (like Flo for Progressive) and they never own their character, it's owned by the brand or the brand's ad agency.

(Almost always the mascot is owned by the brand but there are exceptions; for example, the character Ernest P. Worrell, although depicted by Jim Varney and an endorser of all sorts of products, was created and owned by the agency Carden and Cherry)

You might think that producing 'evergreen' content for your channel will future-proof your traffic and revenue opportunity, but I really believe there's no such thing. Our world moves too fast, especially on YouTube. People's interests fluctuate quite rapidly due to the abundance of information we are now able to access.

Furthermore, YouTube's algorithms themselves favor fresh content. Your channel might be doing well currently, but as you do not control the YouTube platform you are not in control of factors like how discover-able your content is in the future. Just as YouTube has removed features like video sharing, video responses, YT user groups and re-worked its algorithms to favor watch time, YT could suddenly decide to make another big change that kills your traffic from its search engine. Again this has happened to many creators in the past. Worse, YouTube content generally has a really, really long tail because of the competition which makes the value of old videos depreciate over time.

On top of all this YouTube serves ads against pretty much all videos on the platform but the ads are based on advertiser bids against specific keywords, channels, audience categories, etc. YouTube creators ad revenue is largely based on the spending habits of a handful of marketers who purchase large volumes of ads targeting specific demographics. AdWords is honestly more of a wholesale ad platform than a premium one, which makes its long-term value as a revenue source questionable.

If you really want to future proof your career as a content producer I would explore every possible revenue stream and setup portfolios for investing the money. This is all the kind of thing a good rep can help you do, but you can begin the process by learning how to initiate and develop your own brand deals – which is the purpose of this book.

Here are some of the things you can get sponsorships for:

- To underwrite your marketing efforts.
- To cover the expenses of creating blog and e-zine content.
- For providing food and drinks for events you host.
- To acquire product for give-aways and other contests that you hold for your fanbase.
- To cover the costs of travel to conventions, tournaments or other events.
- To fund one or more episodes of content for your channel.

Making Your Brand Attractive to Sponsorships

The most important thing to acquiring sponsorships would be to add value for that potential sponsor. This helps make the deal irresistible to the brand.

Sponsors are searching for target marketplaces that they're attempting to penetrate. Every company has a specific customer profile that they want to focus on marketing to. Your ability to reach that target customer profile is your value to the brand. You should use the data from your YouTube Analytics account to showcase the demographics and social reach of your channel videos, as this will help persuade the brand to do business with you.

Your audience demographic the most important data for locking down a brand deal. If you haven't done so already you should examine your channel's YouTube Statistics to determine the type of individuals who your content is most popular with.

The most 3 important factors of an audience demographic is:

1. Age
2. Gender
3. Location

   1) Age
   If your content attracts males between the age range of 18-24, you will immediately attract the interest of any brand whose customer profile is males within their late-teens and early-twenties. It's that easy.
   2) Audience Size (per video)
   The 2nd critical number you'll need is the audience size per video, also known as your average views-per-video. Usually this number is obtained by reviewing your 5 newest videos and calculating their average views-per-video.
   > NOTE: This differs from your overall subscriber count. Brands are only thinking about the number of individuals who will discover the video where their advertisement can be seen. So although your subscriber count is a number that helps identify how popular your channel may be during its entire lifetime, it isn't always a precise representative of the number of individuals who will actually watch the video you are trying to sell the sponsor on.
   3) Location

While brands can ship products anywhere in the world, generally a product is aimed at customers in specific regions where the brand company has (through internally produced market research) identified the largest opportunity for growth. This is why the viewer location data in your YouTube Analytics dashboard is important to consider and convey to a brand when pitching them. It doesn't do a company who seeks to target audiences in the United States any good if the majority of your audience lives in the Philippines.

Another important consideration is to understand the people who run the marketing divisions at companies are not stupid. They want their company to get their money worth. If you get a $10,000 sponsorship the brand expects to receive $10,000 worth of value; and what brands want more than anything is a quality representation of their brand.

Where many creators go wrong is believing they should be paid large amounts of money for a floating head video filmed on a webcam where you simply endorse someone's product or business. Although brands will pay for this they simply will not pay a lot for it, because it is not a quality showcase of their product.

Developing a Pitch

Awhile back I was having lunch with a friend -- let's call her Nancy -- who asked me for advice on how to raise money for a new web series she wanted to produce.

Nancy is no stranger to producing web shows. She has done it before but she always had to work with bare bones budgets and the shows never produced any money, making it hard for her to work on the next project. Even though she's seasoned at producing for the web, she is struggling to get funding for the next project. This is ultimately because the advice many people have given her is 100% wrong. Many people are still giving advice as if the indie film world hasn't changed in the past decade. Unbelievably, the majority of indie film-makers are still producing pilots on extended credit and doing road-trips to film festivals hoping a distributor takes pity on them. Or they are just dumping their show onto YouTube and crossing their fingers that it goes viral. Some people even think they can get grants.

Stop the madness! This is not how the industry works these days!

Web TV now works the SAME WAY the broadcast TV business works.

In this guide I am going to tell Nancy exactly how to produce her next web series by drafting her a battle plan, and by studying this guide you too will know how to do the same for any web series you want to make.

Step 1) Write a Treatment

Yes, a treatment.

What? You're going to write all 12 episodes of the show in advance before you make any money? Dude, that's a massive waste of time. What if nobody funds your genius show? Then you've spent weeks working on a project that won't make you money.

Oh yes, we're having the money conversation right now and if the words 'SELL OUT' have crossed your mind then you've just confirmed why we need to talk about this subject.

Get your head in the game. Film-making can either be your very expensive hobby or your very lucrative career. You need to decide right now if you want to be a professional who works full-time in the industry while providing for his / her family and leading a fabulous lifestyle, or if you want to be a broke-ass auteur who lives in a van down by the river when she isn't flipping burgers for McDonalds.

Because there are only two routes available for you if you treat film-making like a hobby; broke and alone, or teaching Video Production classes at your local community college.

So yes, you will write a treatment and not a screenplay. Like any professional screenwriter, you will not write a screenplay until someone pays you to do so.

In Nancy's case, her treatment is simple. She wants to produce a show about the people who work at a gaming publisher. Thus her treatment shall be based around the following premise:

"WHAT IF THE CHARACTERS OF THE OFFICE WORKED AT BLIZZARD, AND THERE WAS A STRONGER EMPHASIS ON THE OFFICE ROMANCES?"

This is simple and easy to understand. What kind of shenanigans might then transpire if Michael Scott was in charge of World of Warcraft? Can you imagine Dwight as your unfriendly neighborhood tech support specialist? What if Kevin was the lead programmer? There is vast potential for humor here.

Now here is the more important question:

WHO MIGHT WANT TO SPONSOR THIS SHOW?

Actually, that's the wrong question to ask. Sorry.

Well, Blizzard might. Blizzard could better engage with its customers through a fictional representation of the company. Imagine if Progressive Insurance made a show starring Flo; I'd watch it and so would you. And GEICO did sponsor that Caveman TV Series based on its own commercials so there is some precedence for this in consumer marketing.

Because the show is also a romantic comedy, it may appeal to a dating service like eHarmony; but let's say eHarmony won't go for it. No big deal, there are many other dating services out there and there is a high chance one of them will say yes if the rest of your pitch provides the one thing they want to know: HOW MANY POTENTIAL CUSTOMERS WILL WATCH IT?

In this situation, the customer a dating site most wants to reach is single adult women.

This fact is why the show is going to also be a romantic comedy (remember Pam and Jim, and Dwight and Angela?) and rom-coms appeal primarily to single women.

To understand why a dating site most wants to target single women, let's explore how dating sites operate.

Dating site user-bases are rather lopsided. Men make up the majority of the userbase, and as they are the most aggressive gender in the dating game they need the least convincing to use a dating site. However, dating sites are only profitable if the men are able to actually meet women IRL and go on dates. Even if the relationships do not work out, if the guys actually met women IRL through the site they will continue paying that monthly subscription fee so they can meet more women.

If a guy doesn't get a date through the service in the first month, he will leave the service for a competitor.

Therefore, the bulk of dating site marketing is focused on convincing women to join the service, so that there is always a fresh supply of single ladies to satisfy the legions of overly excited single men.

That is why eHarmony should want to sponsor a rom-com web show. It will make their brand more noticeable to the demographic they most want to engage with.

And your choice of casting should reflect this fact so that eHarmony will give you the money to produce your show.

Step 2) Cast your talent

If I was the casting director, this is how I'd do my casting.....

Michael Scott - Doug Walker
(https://www.youtube.com/user/LeagueOfSu
perCritics)

Jan Levinson - Olga Kay
(https://www.youtube.com/user/olgakay)

Dwight Schrute - Leigh Daniel Avidan
(https://www.youtube.com/user/NinjaSexPar
ty)

Jim Halpert - Arin Hanson
(https://www.youtube.com/user/egoraptor)

Pam Beesly - Lindsay Ellis
(http://blip.tv/nostalgia-chick)

Phyllis Lapin - Antonella
Inserra (http://blip.tv/nostalgia-chick)

Darryl Philbin - DeStorm Power (
https://www.youtube.com/user/DeStorm)

Kevin Malone - Andre Meadows
(https://www.youtube.com/user/BlackNerdC
omedy)

Meredith Palmer - Katie Wilson
(https://www.youtube.com/user/ihavmnyskil
ls)

Angela Martin - Jenna
Marbles https://www.youtube.com/user/Jenna
Marbles

Kelly Kapoor - Franchesca Ramsey
(https://www.youtube.com/user/chescaleigh)

Ryan Howard - Nice Peter
(https://www.youtube.com/user/nicepeter)

Boom, there you go. Millions of folks will watch this show.

These are all web TV celebrities who, I believe, would be capable of performing the role and have large audiences that will appeal to eHarmony and other advertisers.

And by 'role' I don't mean a carbon copy of the original Office characters. I mean fulfilling the ROLE they perform in the story. The backgrounds of the characters will be original, but the relationship dynamics and basic persona of the characters will be the same as their The Office counter-parts.

If you are confused, it's okay. That's what screenwriters are for. Anyone versed in monomyth structure will know what to do, so once you get the show funded you can hire some writers to crank the scripts out.

So, why did I specifically single out the above actors as the cast for this show?

There are three things you are looking for in your casting;

(1) combined audience sizes of the talent,

(2) the demographics of those audiences and,

Many of the actors I selected work together at a website called 'Channel Awesome'. I know that all the Channel Awesome folks like Doug Walker and Lindsay Ellis can work together because they do it all the time, and I know Arin Hanson and Danny Avidan can have a Jim / Dwight style relationship because they already do it on Game Grumps. I also know that many of the other talent have worked in the past with Nice Peter on Epic Rap Battles of History. Andre Meadows and Katie Wilson are also frequent collaborators.

Best of all, almost all of these actors have their own personal YouTube channels. You can actually use a screenshot from their YouTube analytics pages to show your advertisers the precise demographics the talent already possesses on their own shows, and this infers if they all do a show together that their audiences will combine like Voltron.

And if you can't get one of the YouTubers to commit to the show, no big deal. You don't have to get Olga Kay; there are a thousand and one female YouTubers who do the exact same type of comedy she does and have the exact same audience. One of them will take the role Olga Kay turned down so they can brag about it when the show is ultra successful.

Advertisers and investors only care about the demographic reach of the talent, not the talent themselves.

Step 3) Hire your crew

You can cast whoever you want as crew. Really, it doesn't matter.

Okay, sure. Anyone who works in the biz knows that having fantastic crew totally matters a lot. It makes or breaks the production. But the people giving you money do not care about the crew at all because the world's greatest editor and sound guy have no audience to help promote the show.

So really, it doesn't matter who you hire as crew. They don't need to be mentioned in the pitch deck at all. The only thing that matters is the talent and the audience they can bring to the table. Just make sure you hire people who can actually perform their jobs as a professional and produce quality work. Someone might ask to see your Director of Photography's demo reel just to make sure he / she knows how to operate a camera and light a scene, but that's the only reason.

Step 4) Make pitch decks

You need two types of pitch decks; one for advertisers, and one for investors.

Do not confuse the two, as while both will be bankrolling your production, each group have different motivations.

Advertisers are companies like eHarmony. They just want to get more customers to their service through exposure, and (usually) don't really care about receiving a cut of the show's revenue. They are in the business of selling a service or product, not making movies.

Investors are different; they want a cut of the show's profits. They want to put X amount of money into your show and get back Y amount in return.

They both speak similar languages, but investors are much more risk averse than advertisers because the investor uses his / her personal wealth to fund your show, whereas companies will be using a small portion of their overall annual marketing budget so even if the show completely tanks the chances of it causing them financial ruin are slim to none.

This is why you usually need to get advertisers before you can get investors. The absolute ideal situation for an investor is to invest into "growth"; that is, something that has already produced money. If you have advertisers who have already paid you then investors are much more willing to give you more money because it demonstrates growth.

So basically, your advertising deck is going to be like this:

Slide 1: Show treatment and concept

Slide 2: Talent in the show

Slide 3: Audience demographics of the talent

Slide 4: How much money you want from the advertiser for different tiers of promotion, mostly integrated brand sponsorships.

Your deck for investors will be nearly identical to the advertiser deck except you replace Slide 4 with how much money advertisers have already given you and add a fifth slide that explains how much money you are asking from investors and how their money will be returned (for example, a cut of future ad earnings).

If you need a more detailed example of what a pitch deck should look like you can read my blog post, http://careymartell.com/2015/11/how-to-write-a-

Bear in mind, investors should only get a cut of the money for those episodes they actually helped fund.

If you are only raising money for Season 1, do not give them profits from future Seasons. You will need to go back to your original investors for more money when you need to produce Season 2, 3, 4 etc. and if they already get a cut of those seasons they have no incentive to invest again.

Some investors will try to get a slice of licensing rights and so on. Don't give it to them; that's what you as the producing studio need to keep for yourself to turn a profit. The brand needs to belong to you, not someone who gave you a few thousand dollars to produce a dozen episodes.

Identifying the Right Companies

You need to be laser-focused on your Niche – focus on the problem you can solve for a brand. If you primarily produce game reviews on your channel, don't try to seek an endorsement from a beauty company as you will not be able to solve their marketing problem (generating sales from customers of beauty products). Even if some of the demographics of your show are similar to that of the customer profile of the cosmetics company, the simple truth is the fans of your gaming channel are not coming to you for makeup recommendations. Choose the path of least resistance and find a brand that fits the content you make.

Or, alternatively, produce content that you know will be brand friendly.

An important thing to consider is that for major brands their budget primarily goes into traditional forms of marketing, such as the production of television commercials. To secure these sort of projects you might want to consider approaching a creative ad agency who handles these campaigns for the large brand and bid on the contract to produce the commercial. You will need to have setup a production company to do this, and while it would be an excellent form of revenue for you, how to setup a commercial production company falls outside the scope of this book. It is one route to consider which is why I mention it here.

There are thousands of companies out there which can make it difficult to know where to begin. To start the process of narrowing down who your ideal brand clients will be, do the following:

- Create a list of the companies who have a customer profile that fits your channel's audience demographics.
- Produce a pitch towards the specific companies making your offer irresistible.
- Network with the company's representatives to obtain the contact information for the head of marketing who will listen to your pitch.

Networking to Generate Leads

Your ability to cultivate a relationship with the marketing personnel at the company is ultimately what will determine the kind of sponsorship deal you can land. The higher your degree of internal buy-in at the company, the better your deal will be.

However, make sure you are talking to the right people; the decision makers. Due to their inexperience I've seen people waste a lot of time chasing bad leads. For example, someone who works at the IT department at Pepsi has no pull whatsoever in marketing, and despite what they claim probably does not have any ability to make the correct introductions you need.

LinkedIn is a fantastic resource for identifying the people you should be talking to. You can then figure out where they are based, and try to initiate meetings through the messaging system. If that fails you can instead figure out what events they are attending so you can introduce yourself in person.

Over the years I have learned there are a few places that are ideal to find the marketing division employees for a brand;

- Attending trade shows and conventions where the brand has sent employees to generate new business.
- Getting involved in professional networking meetups.
- Visiting office hour functions at a brand's satellite offices.

When you attend these events make sure you bring some promotional materials with you about your channel, show or project; you need not bring an entire pitch deck, but you should have something to help explain what you do.

Primarily you should have business cards. This might seem old-fashioned to some, but let me explain.

Your #1 goal with introducing yourself to a marketing person is to get their email address. The worst thing you can do is get a great rapport going with someone who can champion you inside their company and then have no way to follow up with them after the convention is over. Do not settle for just handing out your card; people can lose it (they can slip out of a pocket while getting their phone or wallet). You want to acquire their business card and the best way to do this is to exchange your own.

During these networking events you should never walk away from someone without asking for their business card. If they do not have a business card you need to pull out a notepad and pen, and get them to write it down (don't write it down yourself; you might mishear and write it down wrong. Cons are noisy places and I've made this mistake in the past).

I really need to stress this: Your business card is more important than your pamphlets. Your business card fits into a pocket easier and is thus much less likely to get lost. I estimate they have 70% more "stickiness" than any other kind of promotional material. You'll still have people lose / toss them, but it's more likely to stay with them than a huge sheet of paper someone has to drag around all day.

Your business card should have your name, title, company, company website, your email address and your phone number. You may also want your FB Page and Twitter, too. The back of your business card should have a QR card taking the person directly to whatever it is you are trying to promote; not everyone will scan it, but many will (some marketers insist QR code usage is a myth. It's not; I've watched people use them).

Believe it or not I have met people from major companies who did not have any business cards. They said it was because they were "new hires", having only worked a couple weeks and the company hadn't issued them any cards yet. These folks had to login to their phone apps and send me an email directly.

This is inexcusable. Anyone can order 500 new cards from Vistaprint for $50. Business cards are insanely easy to acquire and there is no reason to not have some before a major promotional event. If you can pay to attend a convention you can surely pay $50 to get them some business cards.

While attending a convention it can sometimes be difficult to figure out who to talk to. Many conventions have different color coded badges depending on if someone is a regular attendee or a representative for a major brand, and if you can recognize the differences you can introduce yourself to people who are wearing an industry badge. Other than having your own booth at the show, this is the 2nd best thing you can do to generate leads.

If you see someone with an industry badge, then you should ask them who they work for. Remember, their company has sent them to generate new business so it is not rude to do this.

Yes, I am telling you to cold-call people in the real world. This is what separates the successful entrepreneurs from the failures; the ability to talk to anyone and risk rejection. If you can't overcome your fear of rejection you will never take your startup anywhere.

When I attend shows I walk the exhibit floor all day hunting passes and collect hundreds of business cards. I performed 2 minute demos of the app or project using my tablet or laptop. Even after the exhibit halls close, I continue to walk around outside for two hours doing the same thing. These shows often have thousands of attendees and you won't see them all, but you can meet a lot of them if you hunt.

The people you will meet are from companies big and small, but even if someone isn't from a company you are specifically looking for, pitch them anyway. They probably know someone who is your target customer.

I really need to stress this last part; treat everyone with respect. At a past networking events I had a lady approach me and say she was looking for a job as an accountant. She asked me what I did, and as soon as I explained I worked in web television, before I could even hand her my card she turned around abruptly and walked off. Then a week later she saw me at her new boss' office talking to her boss about a deal. I could actually see the surprise on her face when she realized she had been incredibly rude to someone who could have introduced her to the guy who eventually hired her.

You never know who is connected to who. If they are wearing an industry pass, the leads are always good. Be cool to everyone, as you never know where it might lead.

Ideally you should have a team of people with you; you should have people at a booth, and people walking the floors badge hunting. This will allow you to cover a lot more ground.

Email Lead Generation

You can also cold-call brand representatives by sending them an email inquiry. This method doesn't consume any money on your behalf, but it is very time consuming.

You need to remember that starting out you will have to email a lot of brands representatives who know nothing about your channel; you will need to educate them in the email you draft. Many people simply will not respond to you as they won't be interested, but every now and then you may discover a response indicating the marketing department is interested in having a meeting to discuss your proposal. Make sure you have the time and resources needed to make the trip to the brand's headquarters for the meeting; don't expect them to fly you out if you live far away.

You can also use certain websites like FameBit and Grapevine to help you identify companies seeking to pay creators to endorse their products. These services also give you the ability to directly message the brand reps at these companies and submit your pitch proposal.

The Sponsorship Agreement

If you get advertisers and investors who want to give you money, great! Now it's time to do the contracts. Everything must be in writing with clear expectations written in black ink. Verbal agreements and handshakes are not enforceable things. Remember, if it's not in the contract then it doesn't exist.

I am not a lawyer and I am not giving you legal advice. I took a course in paralegal studies during college so I am capable of reading and writing my own contracts, but even I defer to the judgement of lawyers when large amounts of cash start flying around. A decent entertainment lawyer will take their commission fee out of the money you collect from everyone else.

You also need contracts for your talent. It needs to be clear how much they will be paid and what % of any royalties the talent will earn.

If your talent is SAG-AFTRA you're gonna get screwed pretty heavily because the guild's rules are designed for major networks who spend a million dollars an episode whereas you will more likely spend $10,000 an episode. They will try to make you hire all kinds of union people you don't need to produce a TV show these days, and enforce all kinds of stupid rules that will slow down production for you.

   If at all possible avoid hiring union talent and just pay everyone at scale yourself. Inviting union crews into your production will not only increase the costs, but it will also make it harder to swiftly complete the production.

   Your talent's contracts should also require the talent to do promotion for the show, such as sharing the video on social profiles, attending panels at conventions and whatnot. Remember you are hiring the talent specifically because the advertisers want to reach their fanbases. I've heard many horror stories about people producing web shows and hiring big name talent who never once share the show with anyone and it causes the show to fail. Make sure your talent is contractually obligated to promote the show or they don't get paid.

How to Follow Up After the Project is Done

Brands do not want to spend money idly; this is a business deal, after all. You will need to measure the results and show how they benefited the brand's marketing goals.

A **Proof of Performance Report**, or p.o.p. is important for drafting to let the brand know it did not waste its money funding your project and that it should renew the deal to continue reaping the benefits of the deal. For example, you might be able to correlate the rise of a brand's Facebook Page followers with the release of your endorsement video by comparing the release time with the rise in Facebook Page followers.

If you had a link to the brand's website in your video and used a URL shortening service like bit.ly to track each click you can generate a report showing how many new visitors the brand received to its website (a crucial point of sale for many companies) you can demonstrate the value the brand received.

What data is specifically in your p.o.p. is going to be determined largely by the goal the brand wants to achieve from the deal they made with you, and the brand will often set the criteria for measurement themselves.

Conclusion

I hope this guidebook has helped you become informed on the steps necessary for securing a brand deal for your channel from a sponsor. Remember to stay professional in all your dealings with a prospective client (which is what the brands are to you) and fulfil your obligations in the contract.

If you are looking for additional advice related to building a business around a YouTube channel you can find more articles and books I have written on the subject at http://careymartell.com/

www.ingramcontent.com/pod-product-compliance
Lightning Source LLC
Chambersburg PA
CBHW051217050326
40689CB00008B/1344